ANNE GEDDES

1997
Datebook

A COLLECTION OF IMAGES

ISBN 1-55912-235-8

© Anne Geddes 1996

Published in 1996 by Cedco Publishing Company,
2955 Kerner Blvd, San Rafael, CA 94901.
First USA edition 1995.

Produced by Kel Geddes
Color separations by Image Centre
Typesetting by Advision
Printed in Hong Kong

ANNE GEDDES ™

is the registered trademark
of The Especially Kids Company Limited

ANNE GEDDES

Welcome to this new collection of Anne Geddes' images to be enjoyed throughout 1997.

Children provide the inspiration for her outstanding work. She is not sure of why herself, but Anne admits she has spent much time in searching for an answer. "I hope that through my work as a photographer, I have been able to pass on my appreciation of the beauty and charm of little children. As adults, we all need to stop occasionally and look at ourselves and our circumstances with an open mind and a sense of humour, and remember to appreciate the simple things in life, which are often the most important."

Several images from her recently completed book *Down in the Garden* are reproduced in this publication. The book showcases Anne's remarkable imagination, her love of little children and presents in a light-hearted way a special world full of fantasy, fun and laughter.

In Anne's words, "Children are the true believers, and some of us are lucky to make the transition to adulthood without ever losing the ability to see through young eyes."

Thanks to Anne many of us are able to recapture those precious moments through the magic of her images.

Anne's quest for that elusive answer continues and all of us who can share and enjoy the special quality she is able to bring to our lives through her images, hope her search is forever.

Anne is married to her business partner and best friend Kel. Together they have two children.

1997 Calendar

January

S	M	T	W	T	F	S
			1	2	3	4
5	6	7	8	9	10	11
12	13	14	15	16	17	18
19	20	21	22	23	24	25
26	27	28	29	30	31	

February

S	M	T	W	T	F	S
						1
2	3	4	5	6	7	8
9	10	11	12	13	14	15
16	17	18	19	20	21	22
23	24	25	26	27	28	

March

S	M	T	W	T	F	S
						1
2	3	4	5	6	7	8
9	10	11	12	13	14	15
16	17	18	19	20	21	22
23	24	25	26	27	28	29
30	31					

April

S	M	T	W	T	F	S
		1	2	3	4	5
6	7	8	9	10	11	12
13	14	15	16	17	18	19
20	21	22	23	24	25	26
27	28	29	30			

May

S	M	T	W	T	F	S
				1	2	3
4	5	6	7	8	9	10
11	12	13	14	15	16	17
18	19	20	21	22	23	24
25	26	27	28	29	30	31

June

S	M	T	W	T	F	S
1	2	3	4	5	6	7
8	9	10	11	12	13	14
15	16	17	18	19	20	21
22	23	24	25	26	27	28
29	30					

July

S	M	T	W	T	F	S
		1	2	3	4	5
6	7	8	9	10	11	12
13	14	15	16	17	18	19
20	21	22	23	24	25	26
27	28	29	30	31		

August

S	M	T	W	T	F	S
					1	2
3	4	5	6	7	8	9
10	11	12	13	14	15	16
17	18	19	20	21	22	23
24	25	26	27	28	29	30
31						

September

S	M	T	W	T	F	S
	1	2	3	4	5	6
7	8	9	10	11	12	13
14	15	16	17	18	19	20
21	22	23	24	25	26	27
28	29	30				

October

S	M	T	W	T	F	S
		1	2	3	4	
5	6	7	8	9	10	11
12	13	14	15	16	17	18
19	20	21	22	23	24	25
26	27	28	29	30	31	

November

S	M	T	W	T	F	S
						1
2	3	4	5	6	7	8
9	10	11	12	13	14	15
16	17	18	19	20	21	22
23	24	25	26	27	28	29
30						

December

S	M	T	W	T	F	S
	1	2	3	4	5	6
7	8	9	10	11	12	13
14	15	16	17	18	19	20
21	22	23	24	25	26	27
28	29	30	31			

DECEMBER - JANUARY

SUNDAY	29
MONDAY	30
TUESDAY	31
WEDNESDAY *New Year's Day* ◐ *Last Quarter Moon*	1
THURSDAY	2
FRIDAY	3
SATURDAY	4

From Anne's Book *"Down in the Garden"*   *Fiona Butterfly*

JANUARY

| SUNDAY | 5 |

| MONDAY | 6 |

| TUESDAY | 7 |

| WEDNESDAY | 8 |

●
New Moon

| THURSDAY | 9 |

| FRIDAY | 10 |

| SATURDAY | 11 |

JANUARY

SUNDAY 12

MONDAY 13

TUESDAY 14

WEDNESDAY 15

◐
First Quarter Moon

THURSDAY 16

FRIDAY 17

SATURDAY 18

JANUARY

SUNDAY	19
MONDAY *Martin Luther King Jr. Day*	20
TUESDAY	21
WEDNESDAY	22
THURSDAY ○ *Full Moon*	23
FRIDAY	24
SATURDAY	25

JANUARY - FEBRUARY

SUNDAY	26
MONDAY	27
TUESDAY	28
WEDNESDAY	29
THURSDAY	30
FRIDAY	31

◑ *Last Quarter Moon*

SATURDAY	1

Julia Snail

FEBRUARY

SUNDAY	2
MONDAY	3
TUESDAY	4
WEDNESDAY	5
THURSDAY	6
FRIDAY	7

● *New Moon*

SATURDAY	8

FEBRUARY

SUNDAY	9
MONDAY	10
TUESDAY	11
WEDNESDAY *Lincoln's Birthday* *Ash Wednesday*	12
THURSDAY	13
FRIDAY *St. Valentine's Day* ◐ *First Quarter Moon*	14
SATURDAY	15

FEBRUARY

SUNDAY	16
MONDAY *Presidents' Day*	17
TUESDAY	18
WEDNESDAY	19
THURSDAY	20
FRIDAY	21
SATURDAY *Washington's Birthday* ○ *Full Moon*	22

FEBRUARY - MARCH

SUNDAY	23
MONDAY	24
TUESDAY	25
WEDNESDAY	26
THURSDAY	27
FRIDAY	28
SATURDAY	1

ANNE GEDDES

From Anne's Book "Down in the Garden"

MARCH

SUNDAY	2

◑
Last Quarter Moon

MONDAY Psych Care Plan Due	3

TUESDAY	4

WEDNESDAY	5

THURSDAY	6

FRIDAY	7

SATURDAY *International Women's Day*	8

●
New Moon

MARCH

SUNDAY	9
MONDAY	10
TUESDAY	11
WEDNESDAY	12
THURSDAY	13
FRIDAY	14
SATURDAY	15

First Quarter Moon

MARCH

SUNDAY	16
MONDAY *St. Patrick's Day*	17
TUESDAY	18
WEDNESDAY	19
THURSDAY *Vernal Equinox* *8:56 AM E.S.T.*	20
FRIDAY	21
SATURDAY	22

MARCH

SUNDAY *Palm Sunday* ○ *Full Moon*	23
MONDAY	24
TUESDAY	25
WEDNESDAY	26
THURSDAY	27
FRIDAY *Good Friday*	28
SATURDAY	29

MARCH - APRIL

SUNDAY *Easter*	**30**
MONDAY ◑ *Last Quarter Moon*	**31**
TUESDAY	**1**
WEDNESDAY	**2**
THURSDAY	**3**
FRIDAY	**4**
SATURDAY	**5**

APRIL

SUNDAY *Daylight Saving Time* *begins in U.S.A.* *(Add 1 hour to clock)*	6
MONDAY ● *New Moon*	7
TUESDAY	8
WEDNESDAY	9
THURSDAY	10
FRIDAY	11
SATURDAY	12

APRIL

SUNDAY	13
MONDAY	14

◐
First Quarter Moon

TUESDAY	15
WEDNESDAY	16
THURSDAY	17
FRIDAY	18
SATURDAY	19

APRIL

SUNDAY	20

MONDAY *Passover* *(begins at sunset)*	21

TUESDAY *Earth Day* ○ *Full Moon*	22

WEDNESDAY	23

THURSDAY	24

FRIDAY *National Arbor Day*	25

SATURDAY	26

ANNE GEDDES

APRIL - MAY

| SUNDAY | 27 |

| MONDAY | 28 |

| TUESDAY | 29 |

◐
Last Quarter Moon

| WEDNESDAY | 30 |

| THURSDAY | 1 |

| FRIDAY | 2 |

| SATURDAY | 3 |

MAY

SUNDAY	4
MONDAY	5
TUESDAY	6

●
New Moon

WEDNESDAY	7
THURSDAY	8
FRIDAY	9
SATURDAY	10

MAY

SUNDAY
Mother's Day

11

MONDAY

12

TUESDAY

13

WEDNESDAY

14

◑
First Quarter Moon

THURSDAY

15

FRIDAY

16

SATURDAY

17

ANNE GEDDES

MAY

SUNDAY *Pentecost*	**18**
MONDAY *Victoria Day* *(Canada)*	**19**
TUESDAY	**20**
WEDNESDAY	**21**
THURSDAY ○ *Full Moon*	**22**
FRIDAY	**23**
SATURDAY	**24**

MAY

SUNDAY	25
MONDAY *Memorial Day*	26
TUESDAY	27
WEDNESDAY	28
THURSDAY ◑ *Last Quarter Moon*	29
FRIDAY	30
SATURDAY	31

JUNE

SUNDAY	1
MONDAY	2
TUESDAY	3
WEDNESDAY	4
THURSDAY	5
● New Moon	
FRIDAY	6
SATURDAY	7

ANNE GEDDES

From Anne's Book "Down in the Garden"

JUNE

SUNDAY	8
MONDAY	9
TUESDAY	10
WEDNESDAY	11
THURSDAY	12
FRIDAY	13

◐
First Quarter Moon

SATURDAY	14

Flag Day

ANNE GEDDES

JUNE

SUNDAY
Father's Day

15

MONDAY

16

TUESDAY

17

WEDNESDAY

18

THURSDAY

19

FRIDAY

20

○
Full Moon

SATURDAY
Summer Solstice
4:21 AM E.D.T.

21

JUNE

SUNDAY
22

MONDAY
23

TUESDAY
St. Jean Baptiste Day
(Quebec)
24

WEDNESDAY
25

THURSDAY
26

FRIDAY
27

◐
Last Quarter Moon

SATURDAY
28

JUNE - JULY

SUNDAY	29
MONDAY	30
TUESDAY *Canada Day*	1
WEDNESDAY	2
THURSDAY	3
FRIDAY *Independence Day* ● *New Moon*	4
SATURDAY	5

ANNE GEDDES

From Anne's Book "Down in the Garden"
"Sweet Peas"

JULY

SUNDAY	6
MONDAY	7
TUESDAY	8
WEDNESDAY	9
THURSDAY	10
FRIDAY	11
SATURDAY	12

◑
First Quarter Moon

ANNE GEDDES

JULY

SUNDAY	13
MONDAY	14
TUESDAY	15
WEDNESDAY	16
THURSDAY	17
FRIDAY	18
SATURDAY	19

○
Full Moon

JULY

SUNDAY	20
MONDAY	21
TUESDAY	22
WEDNESDAY	23
THURSDAY	24
FRIDAY	25
SATURDAY	26

◑
Last Quarter Moon

ANNE GEDDES

JULY - AUGUST

SUNDAY	27
MONDAY	28
TUESDAY	29
WEDNESDAY	30
THURSDAY	31
FRIDAY	1
SATURDAY	2

AUGUST

SUNDAY	3

●
New Moon

MONDAY	4
TUESDAY	5
WEDNESDAY	6
THURSDAY	7
FRIDAY	8
SATURDAY	9

ANNE GEDDES

AUGUST

SUNDAY   10

MONDAY   11

◐
First Quarter Moon

TUESDAY   12

WEDNESDAY   13

THURSDAY   14

FRIDAY   15

SATURDAY   16

ANNE GEDDES

From Anne's Book "Down in the Garden"

AUGUST

SUNDAY	17
MONDAY	18

○
Full Moon

TUESDAY	19
WEDNESDAY	20
THURSDAY	21
FRIDAY	22
SATURDAY	23

ANNE GEDDES

AUGUST

SUNDAY

24

◗
Last Quarter Moon

MONDAY

25

TUESDAY

26

WEDNESDAY

27

THURSDAY

28

FRIDAY

29

SATURDAY

30

AUGUST - SEPTEMBER

SUNDAY

31

MONDAY

Labor Day

●

New Moon

1

TUESDAY

2

WEDNESDAY

3

THURSDAY

4

FRIDAY

5

SATURDAY

6

Field Mice

SEPTEMBER

SUNDAY
Grandparents' Day

7

MONDAY

8

TUESDAY

9

◐
First Quarter Moon

WEDNESDAY

10

THURSDAY

11

FRIDAY

12

SATURDAY

13

SEPTEMBER

SUNDAY — 14

MONDAY — 15

~~complete~~ assignment #2: Prof. Role
Rd. Marriner - Tomey, Ch. 2 & 3

Rd. Michael, 27-55 : CC iv.

TUESDAY — 16

Med. Surg., ~~Ch. 43 & 44~~; review
~~Ch. 10 of SOS~~
~~Ropp 86-111 : CC iv.~~

○
Full Moon

WEDNESDAY — 17

~~finish~~ SOS
get Pt: care plan etc

THURSDAY — 18

finish preparing for clinical
~~note~~ 36-45 : CC iv

FRIDAY — 19

SATURDAY — 20

SEPTEMBER

SUNDAY	21
MONDAY *Autumnal Equinox* *7:57 PM E.D.T.*	22
TUESDAY ◐ *Last Quarter Moon*	23
WEDNESDAY	24
THURSDAY	25
FRIDAY	26
SATURDAY	27

ANNE GEDDES

SEPTEMBER - OCTOBER

SUNDAY	28

MONDAY	29

TUESDAY	30

WEDNESDAY   1
Rosh Hashanah
(begins at sunset)

●
New Moon

THURSDAY	2

FRIDAY	3

SATURDAY	4

Woodland Fairy

OCTOBER

SUNDAY	5
MONDAY	6
TUESDAY	7
WEDNESDAY	8
THURSDAY	9

◑
First Quarter Moon

FRIDAY	10

Yom Kippur
(begins at sunset)

SATURDAY	11

OCTOBER

SUNDAY	12

MONDAY *Columbus Day* *Thanksgiving Day* *(Canada)*	13

TUESDAY	14

WEDNESDAY ○ *Full Moon*	15

THURSDAY	16

FRIDAY	17

SATURDAY	18

ANNE GEDDES

OCTOBER

SUNDAY	19
MONDAY	20
TUESDAY	21
WEDNESDAY	22
THURSDAY	23

◑
Last Quarter Moon

FRIDAY	24
SATURDAY	25

From Anne's Book "Down in the Garden"
"Slipper Orchid"

OCTOBER - NOVEMBER

SUNDAY
Daylight Saving Time
ends in U.S.A.
(subtract 1 hour from clock)

26

MONDAY

27

TUESDAY

28

WEDNESDAY

29

THURSDAY

30

FRIDAY
Halloween

●
New Moon

31

SATURDAY

1

NOVEMBER

SUNDAY 2

MONDAY 3

TUESDAY 4
Election Day

WEDNESDAY 5

THURSDAY 6

FRIDAY 7

◑
First Quarter Moon

SATURDAY 8

NOVEMBER

SUNDAY	9
MONDAY	10
TUESDAY *Veterans Day* *Remembrance Day* *(Canada)*	11
WEDNESDAY	12
THURSDAY	13
FRIDAY ○ *Full Moon*	14
SATURDAY	15

NOVEMBER

SUNDAY	16
MONDAY	17
TUESDAY	18
WEDNESDAY	19
THURSDAY	20
FRIDAY	21

◑
Last Quarter Moon

SATURDAY	22

NOVEMBER

SUNDAY	23
MONDAY	24
TUESDAY	25
WEDNESDAY	26
THURSDAY *Thanksgiving Day*	27
FRIDAY	28
SATURDAY	29

● New Moon

NOVEMBER - DECEMBER

SUNDAY	30
MONDAY	1
TUESDAY	2
WEDNESDAY	3
THURSDAY	4
FRIDAY	5
SATURDAY	6

From Anne's Book "The Twelve Days of Christmas"

A Partridge in a Pear Tree

DECEMBER

SUNDAY	7

◑
First Quarter Moon

MONDAY	8

TUESDAY	9

WEDNESDAY	10

THURSDAY	11

FRIDAY	12

SATURDAY	13

○
Full Moon

ANNE GEDDES

From Anne's Book "The Twelve Days of Christmas"

Nine Ladies Dancing

DECEMBER

SUNDAY	14
MONDAY	15
TUESDAY	16
WEDNESDAY	17
THURSDAY	18
FRIDAY	19
SATURDAY	20

From Anne's Book "The Twelve Days of Christmas"   "Eight Maids a Milking"

DECEMBER

SUNDAY
Winter Solstice
3:09 PM E.S.T.

◑
Last Quarter Moon

21

MONDAY

22

TUESDAY
Hanukkah
(begins at sunset)

23

WEDNESDAY

24

THURSDAY
Christmas Day

25

FRIDAY
Boxing Day
(Canada)

26

SATURDAY

27

ANNE GEDDES

DECEMBER - JANUARY

SUNDAY	28

MONDAY	29

●
New Moon

TUESDAY	30

WEDNESDAY	31

THURSDAY	1
New Year's Day	

FRIDAY	2

SATURDAY	3

ANNE GEDDES

Notes

Notes